NO FEAR

PAGES FROM MY
MINDBOOK
LeoChi

POETRY FROM AN UNKNOWN ARTIST

Demii Unsylie

PAGES FROM MY MINDBOOK BY LEOCHI

This anthology showcases the thought-provoking poetry of Demii Unsylie, also known as the artist LeoChi. Through his unique lens, Demii explores the complexities of human experience, reflecting on themes of identity, belonging, love, and social dynamics. Each poem captures a moment, a feeling, or a truth that resonates deeply with readers, inviting them to see the world through his eyes.

With a style that blends introspection and vivid imagery, Demii's work delves into the nuances of life's struggles and joys. His voice is both relatable and profound, offering insights that challenge perceptions and inspire contemplation. From the depths of personal conflict to the celebration of shared experiences, Demii Unsylie's poetry is a testament to the power of words to connect, heal, and illuminate the human condition.

TABLE OF CONTENTS

SILENT WITNESS

Beneath the pulse of neon lights,

In coffee breaks and shared midnight sighs,

I wear my heart like a hidden scar,

Bruised in places only I know how to find.

You laugh in shadows where I cannot reach,

A melody playing for a different ear,

I trace the curve of your smile in stolen glances,

Dancing with secrets I'll never speak.

Your world spins far from my orbit's pull,

In colors I'll never understand,

But still, I linger in the quiet spaces,

A ghost chasing what can never be.

She holds your heart where I can't compete,

And I, a dreamer tangled in impossible skies,

Love you from a distance, through fleeting touches,

Knowing I'm just a flicker in your firefly eyes.

And still, I return to the warmth of my vows,

A love that breathes freely, not bound to one.

Pan in my soul, poly in my skin,

I wander these streets with a heart that holds more.

Yet, in your smile, I lose myself,

In the way you glow for someone else,

Freedom may cradle my open heart,

But in your orbit, I'll forever burn.

No chains in love, yet still I ache,

To be the moon you cannot see.

I'm free to roam, but tethered still,

A silent witness to the stars we'll never be.

DULL FANGS

Once, my hands were claws,

Tearing through canvas, paper, and sound—

Feral in my hunger, devouring the world,

Turning it into art with wild, sharpened teeth.

But now, I stand before a blank page,

And the beast inside me is quiet,

His roar turned to a whisper,

His fangs dull, slipping from my grip.

I used to carve with a savage grace,

Bleeding colors that screamed my name,

Now I'm a shadow of my old self,

A predator who's forgotten the taste of prey.

What is a beast without his bite?

What is an artist without his flame?

I gnash at the air, hoping for a spark,

But all I catch is silence, a dull ache in my jaw.

The world still spins in vivid hues,

But my claws are soft, my howl a whimper,

I chase the muse through empty forests,

But she's gone, leaving only echoes in her wake.

Still, I stand in the twilight of my craft,

Waiting for the moon to rise again,

To sharpen my teeth on the night's edge,

And find the savage beauty buried within.

I'll sharpen these dull fangs

FIREFLY EYES

You walk through the world, unaware,

Of the way the night bends to your light.

In your quiet gaze, the stars fade,

And I, lost in the glow you can't see.

You hide behind shadows, thinking yourself plain,

But your beauty flickers in ways you don't understand.

Like fireflies that dance in the dark,

Only seen by those who know where to look.

Your laugh is soft, like whispered rain,

Falling in moments you think no one hears.

But I hear it—a melody that lingers,

A song that brightens my skies.

You tuck your smile away,

Believing it belongs to others more deserving.

But in my eyes, you're radiant,

Lighting fires in places you never wander.

If only you could see what I see,

How your presence quietly commands the room,

How your firefly eyes hold a magic,

That makes even the moon seem dull.

And though you belong to a world I can't enter,

I still burn, silently, in your orbit.

Because even from the shadows,

You're the brightest thing in my sky.

You there with the firefly eyes.

RED CIRCLE

We were not born of the same roots,

But bled from the same storms.

In the shadow of forgotten promises, we found each other,

Not by blood, but by the wounds they left behind.

They spoke of duty, yet turned their backs,

Offered hands only to let them slip away.

We learned to stitch our own skin together,

To stand in the spaces where they failed to appear.

Water flows, weak and thin,

But the blood we share runs deeper, unseen,

Drawn not from lineage, but from loyalty,

Crafted in the fires of betrayal's sting.

The womb gave us nothing but hollow words,

And cold, absent eyes that never looked our way.

We built this circle from the broken pieces,

From shards of trust, they left scattered in the dark.

We are not bound by their mistakes,

Nor shackled by the ghosts of their neglect.

We are forged in the furnace of survival,

In the heat of choosing who we stand beside.

This circle is our sanctuary,

A place where disappointment holds no weight,

Where the scars of the past turn to armor,

And the whispers of the false cannot reach.

Let them speak of bonds they abandoned,

Of ties they forgot to nurture.

We rise in spite of them,

Blood of the coven, chosen and strong.

Here, we are more than the family we lost,

More than the wounds they left behind.

We are the flame that never dies,

The red circle, drawn in fire and defiance.

Together, unbroken, we rewrite the story,

Not born of neglect, but of our own power.

In the red circle, we claim our fate,

Not given, but made, as we rise beyond.

In our red circle

TOMORROW'S END

If it all ended tomorrow,

And the sun set on the path we've walked,

I'd hold the moments in my hands like treasure,

Grateful for the laughter we shared in the quiet corners of our days.

If it all ended tomorrow,

And your smile became a memory, not a daily light,

I'd still trace the lines of every conversation,

Knowing your words shaped me in ways I never expected.

If it all ended tomorrow,

And this friendship was all we'd ever be,

I'd carry no regret, only the warmth of your presence,

The gentle fire you sparked in places I didn't know could glow.

If it all ended tomorrow,

And I never got closer than these stolen moments,

I'd be thankful for the way you saw me,

In ways no one else dared to see.

If it all ended tomorrow,

And the silence between us grew long,

I'd smile, remembering how you let me linger,

In your orbit, even though I could never stay.

If it all ended tomorrow,

And you chose another path far from mine,

I'd still carry your light in my heart,

Grateful for the time you gifted, even when it wasn't meant to last.

If it all ended tomorrow,

I would not mourn what never came,

But celebrate what we were, fleeting as it was,

A spark that lit my world, even if just for a while.

If it all ended ...

BLU

In the cold light, where truth is hidden,

We were born into fractures—

The cracks ran deep, but so did we,

Cousins by chance, siblings by choice.

The blue of their blood meant nothing,

When the silence between us ran deeper.

They built walls from neglect,

But we found doorways in the dark.

They could never see the threads we wove,

Silent, beneath their shouting,

A web of loyalty spun from everything they weren't,

In the blue veins of our shared survival.

We didn't need their warmth,

We learned to breathe in the chill they left behind.

Their hands fumbled where ours found strength,

Carving a path, they could never follow.

Cousins? No.

We are the keepers of what they forgot,

The shadow and the light they failed to see.

We spoke without words, built in the spaces between their ruins.

Where they faltered, we stood still,

In the quiet rebellion of our bond,

Not of blood, but of ice,

Stronger for the cracks that tried to break us.

Gratitude is a blade, sharpened on the edge of their absence.

We didn't need their approval,

We only needed each other,

And in the blue of night, we became more.

Let them say we were born into the same storm,

But it's our calm they could never understand.

We are not bound by their mistakes,

We are blue veins, running deep, running true.

AGAINST THE GRAIN

I walk the edges, always just beyond the fold,

A shadow flitting in the corners of laughter,

Where the warmth wraps tight around the chosen,

And I stand, a lone wolf, howling in the dark.

Some days, I slip into the fold,

A heartbeat in sync with the pack,

But just as quickly, I feel the thread unravel,

The weight of my difference pulls me back to the edge.

Their smiles are a language I can't decipher,

Jokes told in whispers, secrets shared in silence.

I'm the outsider with a heart full of questions,

Trying to find my place in a world that won't fit.

I am the black sheep, the frayed thread in their tapestry,

A shape that doesn't quite conform to the weave.

I wear their love like a loose coat,

Fitting in the seams but never quite whole.

In the mirror, I see the wolf staring back,

Fierce and wild yet yearning for connection.

But the pack runs on, chasing dreams I can't touch,

While I linger, a ghost in their joyous hunt.

Each family gathering is a dance of masks,

Their faces bright, mine cloaked in shadows,

Where I navigate the laughter like a maze,

Searching for the exit to a place where I belong.

I carry the weight of belonging like a stone,

Heavy and cold, lodged in the pit of my chest.

What does it mean to be part of the grain,

When I'm constantly pushing against the flow?

Yet in this struggle, I find my voice,

A howl that echoes through the night,

For even lone wolves can carve their paths,

And redefine the meaning of family in their flight.

So, I walk the edges, proud in my difference,

Embracing the solitude that shapes my truth.

For I am against the grain,

And in my heart, I am enough.

CHASING LIGHTS

In the flicker of red and blue,

I feel the weight of eyes,

Each flash a reminder of the hunt,

Where acceptance hangs by a thread, frayed and thin.

A heartbeat away from suspicion,

Every step a dance on the edge,

Where the wrong word can echo like a gunshot,

Branding me forever,

A mark too heavy to wear.

I learned young, in the silence of the streets,

That the language of my body spoke louder than my voice,

Yet no one was there to teach the rules—

The delicate balance between desire and danger,

Where a smile can shift to a snare.

They see the boy in me, but not the man,

Judging the shadow, not the heart,

A monster born from misunderstanding,

Innocence lost in a world that spins on fear,

Where complexity is wrapped in armor, unseen.

Chasing lights, I tread softly,

Mindful of every glance, every laugh,

A misstep could turn joy to judgment,

Turning brotherhood into a battle,

And laughter into whispers behind closed doors.

I walk this tightrope, fraying beneath my weight,

Straddling the line between hope and despair,

As I navigate the alleys of acceptance,

Finding comfort in the shadows,

Yet longing for the light that always seems out of reach.

In the chaos, I seek connection,

But find only flickers of recognition,

Fleeting moments where I am seen,

And then swallowed by the void,

Chasing lights that flicker and fade.

So here I stand, against the glow,

A figure in the night, caught in the beams,

Fighting for a space where I can breathe,

Where my voice is not a threat but a song,

And my heart, a compass that points to home.

Forever chasing lights.

THE GARDEN

In the garden of tomorrow,

I stand, hands trembling,

Tending to petals unfurling,

Wondering if I've watered them right.

You bloom in shades I never knew existed,

A wildflower dancing in a storm,

And I, the keeper of fragile dreams,

Fear the winds will tear you from my grip.

Each day is a canvas,

Painted in hues of doubt and hope,

As I trace the lines of your laughter,

A melody echoing through the chaos,

A symphony of who you are becoming.

I watch as you chase the sun,

Your spirit unfettered, radiant,

Yet the shadows of this world creep in,

And I stumble, uncertain in my steps,

Wishing to shield you from the tempest.

With every tear, a lesson learned,

With every smile, a bridge built,

But do my hands offer enough?

As you weave through thorns and whispers,

I wonder if my roots are strong enough to hold.

You rise, a phoenix from the ashes of yesterday,

Turning pain into strength,

While I stand in awe,

Feeling the weight of my own fears,

Yet buoyed by the beauty of your flight.

In the quiet moments, I find my solace,

In the soft glow of your dreams,

As I let go of the need to control,

And embrace the wonder of your journey,

Knowing love is the compass guiding us both.

So here I am, the gardener of your becoming,

Holding my breath as you reach for the stars,

In this ever-changing landscape,

Where wrong turns are just part of the dance,

And I find joy in watching you blossom,

A testament to the love we share.

BETWEEN THE LINES

You stand in the margins,

A silhouette in borrowed colors,

Just another shade of wheat,

A spirit woven from threads of many tales,

Yet you feel like an echo in a crowded room.

You get the references, the rhythms of the streets,

The jokes that fly like firecrackers,

But you're just a shadow on the edges,

Watching the dance unfold,

Yet never quite stepping into the light.

In a world that thrives on labels,

You wear yours like a second skin,

But it never fits right,

A suit tailored for someone else,

While you fumble through the seams,

Searching for threads that bind.

You navigate the language like a tourist,

Fluent in the lingo, yet foreign in the heart,

A soul caught in the crossfire,

Longing to be embraced,

But always one step away from the warmth.

What does it mean to belong,

When the mirror reflects a face

That feels fragmented, incomplete?

You laugh at the jokes, but the punchlines slip,

Falling flat on the ground where you stand,

Half a heartbeat away from the rhythm.

You watch the world unfold in vibrant hues,

A tapestry woven with stories and strength,

Yet you're a thread pulled too tight,

Barely holding on, longing for the weave,

To find your place among the colors,

To feel the embrace of a culture that's home.

So here you are, a black sheep in the flock,

Dancing to the beat of your own heart,

Yet craving the warmth of a thousand voices,

Hoping one day to step beyond the lines,

And find the rhythm that calls you back,

To a place where you can finally belong.

THROUGH THEIR EYES

Now that I stand in the shadow of parenthood,

I see the world through your weary eyes,

Navigating storms, you faced alone,

With no manual, no map to guide the way.

Each day a tightrope,

Balancing love and fear,

As I juggle the weight of your lessons,

Remembering the echoes of your voice,

Yet feeling the tremor of my own uncertainty.

I thought I knew the burdens you carried,

The heavy sighs behind closed doors,

But now, I grasp the fragility of a child's survival,

The delicate thread that holds us together,

Woven from hopes, dreams, and whispered fears.

Mistakes loom like shadows,

Familiar paths I find myself treading,

Easily echoing the words that cut deep,

The gestures that linger like ghosts,

Haunting my attempts to do better.

But in this chaos, I learn to forgive,

For the moments I misunderstood,

When love was cloaked in exhaustion,

When guidance felt like a weight too heavy to bear.

Now I see the strength it took to rise,

To face the dawn with a heart full of worries,

The delicate balance of holding on and letting go,

And the love that persevered through every trial.

With each challenge I meet,

I honor the battles you fought,

Recognizing the struggle behind every choice,

And the grace it took to hold me close,

Even when the world felt too much.

Now, as I forge my own path,

I carry your lessons like armor,

Learning to navigate the same jagged roads,

With a heart open to understanding,

And hands steady in the face of the storm.

For in this journey of parenthood,

I find echoes of you in my laughter,

And traces of your wisdom in my tears,

A delicate dance of love and resilience,

Binding us together,

In ways we never knew we could be.

IN THE SHADOW OF GREATNESS

In the shadow of greatness, I stand,

A flickering flame beneath the brilliance,

Cousins and siblings rise like constellations,

While I drift, a lone star lost in the void.

I carry the weight of their triumphs,

Millionaire dreams woven into the fabric of my blood,

Doctors and therapists shining like beacons,

Their paths illuminated, while mine remains dim.

Each family gathering, a gallery of success,

Where laughter echoes off the walls of achievement,

And I search for my reflection in their glow,

But find only the shadow of my unfulfilled potential.

I am the eldest, yet feel like the child,

Trapped in the twilight of expectations,

Reaching for greatness that dances just beyond my grasp,

Like a mirage teasing the thirsty soul.

My dreams are whispers, secrets held too tightly,

As if the universe conspires to keep them at bay,

I stand at the precipice of opportunity,

But every leap feels like a stumble in the dark.

What is it to be on the verge of greatness,

Yet feel the cool breeze of inadequacy?

A fingertip away from the life-changing spark,

Yet tethered to the ground by threads of doubt.

In the quiet moments, I question my worth,

Wrestling with the ghosts of ambition unfulfilled,

Fighting against the tide of comparison,

And the echo of voices that say, "Not enough."

But somewhere in this tempest of thought,

A flicker of resilience ignites within,

A reminder that my journey is mine alone,

Not measured by their success, but by my own heartbeat.

So, I'll stand here, in the shadow of greatness,

Finding strength in the struggle,

Learning to embrace the path I carve,

With every step, inching closer to the light,

Knowing that greatness is not just in the destination,

But in the courage to keep reaching,

Even when it feels just out of reach.

One day I'll catch that greatness

IN YOUR EMBRACE

In the quiet corners of our days,

I find solace in your unwavering grace,

A lighthouse in the storm,

Guiding me home when the waves crash high.

You are the patience that calms my fears,

The whisper of understanding when words fail,

In the dance of our lives, you lead with love,

Crafting a rhythm where we both can thrive.

Through trials that tried to pull us apart,

You stood firm, a fortress built on trust,

Your strength a balm for the wounds I hide,

Holding me close when the world felt too much.

I've stumbled and fumbled, lost in the dark,

Yet you never held my mistakes against me,

Instead, you wrapped me in compassion's embrace,

Reminding me of the warrior I can be.

In every fall, you've been my anchor,

A gentle hand lifting me to my feet,

With each reminder of my hidden strength,

You weave a tapestry of hope in my heart.

Together we've built a foundation of love,

Bricks of laughter, mortar of shared dreams,

And as I look into your eyes, I see the light,

A reflection of the man I strive to be.

So here I stand, grateful for your spirit,

For the way you dance through life's tangled threads,

Your love is the compass that guides my way,

In the beautiful chaos that we both create.

With every heartbeat, I cherish you more,

In this journey, hand in hand we'll roam,

For in the light of your strength, I find my own,

Forever grateful, my heart is your home.

TIES THAT BIND

In the tangled roots of our beginnings,

I stood as the sentinel of shadows,

But the weight of the world slipped through my fingers,

As you wandered into the depths of the night.

I wore the armor of a brother's love,

Yet I faltered in the storms we faced,

While you chased whispers in the dark,

Blind to the thorns that waited in silence.

Like a lighthouse dimmed by the fog,

I struggled to shine, to guide your way,

But my light flickered, waning in the chaos,

And I watched as you sailed into tempestuous seas.

We danced on the edge of innocence,

But I misstepped, tripped on my own fears,

While you chased the flickers of a fading flame,

Not knowing the shadows were hungry for more.

In the alleys of regret, I search for answers,

Wondering if my silence sealed your fate,

As you spiraled down paths uncharted,

Where hope dissolved in the ink of despair.

I thought I could weave a tapestry of protection,

But the threads unraveled, frayed by my hands,

Leaving you exposed to the winds of fortune,

Caught in a storm where I couldn't reach.

Now, as you drift in a labyrinth of echoes,

I stand on the edge, a ghost of what could have been,

Carrying the weight of a brother's promise,

Yet feeling the distance stretch like an endless road.

What ties us now, when the bond feels broken?

A threadbare connection that frays with each tear,

But I hold onto the whispers of love,

In hopes that one day, we'll find our way back.

For in the silence between us,

Lies the truth of our shared struggle,

And though I failed to shield you from the storm,

The ties that bind us still pulse with life.

SKIP

In the quiet, shadows shift,

Familiar faces morph into masks,

Once trusted, now they reveal their edges,

The glint of knives hidden beneath smiles.

I stood on the precipice,

Believing in the warmth of your light,

But you wrapped your intentions in honeyed words,

As I slipped, unaware, into your carefully laid traps.

A sibling's laughter that echoed like a bell,

But the chime became a warning,

A toll for innocence lost,

As you cast my name into the storm,

Turning my light to shadows.

In the office where camaraderie thrived,

You wielded words like weapons,

Dismantling my confidence,

A puppeteer pulling strings,

While I danced on the stage of your making.

And the friend who offered a hand,

An outstretched palm cloaked in deceit,

Led me down a path of thorns disguised as roses,

Where my heart bled and my spirit faltered,

Each step a betrayal, each misstep a lesson.

Yet in this tangled web of broken trust,

I find the fibers of my strength,

For every fall was a seed sown,

Every bruise a reminder of the fight within.

These betrayals, though bitter, are the bricks of my ascent,

Building pathways to greatness,

Each cut and scrape a scar of survival,

Proof that I've walked through the fire unyielding.

I gather the shards of my shattered faith,

Turning pain into the fuel of transformation,

For in the wreckage of what once was,

I find the clarity to forge ahead.

So thank you for the lessons wrapped in disguise,

For every moment of doubt, every whispered lie,

You were the catalyst in my growth,

A stepping stone to the heights I now seek.

In the end, betrayal was a bitter gift,

A bitter pill swallowed for the sake of my rise,

And I emerge, stronger, unbroken,

Ready to step into the light.

GREAT BUFFALO

In the tapestry of memory, you stand,

The great buffalo, a spirit untamed,

With a beauty that eclipsed the sun,

And a laugh that danced through the air like a melody.

I held you on a pedestal,

Each flaw hidden beneath layers of light,

Your eyes—two galaxies spinning,

Drawing me in with their enchanting glow.

You were perfection in the autumn haze,

A vibrant leaf caught in the wind's embrace,

I marveled at your brilliance,

Blind to the storms that brewed beneath the surface.

Through rose-colored glasses, I saw the world,

Every moment a brushstroke of bliss,

And I chased the fleeting shadows of your smile,

Believing we were destined to wander together.

But time, the patient teacher, revealed the truth,

In the quiet spaces between our laughter,

I learned that not all that glitters is gold,

And love can be a mirage in the desert of desire.

You were a vision, yes, but also a storm,

With a heart that danced to its own beat,

And I, the moth drawn to your flame,

Burned in the brilliance that was never meant to last.

Now, in the rearview of my life,

I see the beauty in the imperfections,

How the light and shadow painted our story,

Crafting lessons from the heartache of what could have been.

I understand why the universe sighed,

Why fate drew the curtain on our stage,

For sometimes, the great buffalo is not meant to be caught,

But rather to roam free in the wilds of memory.

And while you remain a ghost in my heart,

A whisper of love lost in the winds of time,

I've learned to cherish the moments we shared,

Knowing that perfection was a dream I crafted alone.

So here's to you, the great buffalo,

A symbol of love and longing,

May you run wild and free in the echoes of my soul,

Forever remembered, yet never mine to hold.

TO THE UNSUNG

In the quiet corners of my journey,

Where shadows loom and doubts take flight,

You stood as beacons in the fog,

Unsung heroes, igniting my light.

For every moment when I faltered,

You saw the spark beneath the ash,

Whispering faith when my own voice trembled,

Believing in dreams that felt like a distant flash.

You took a chance when the path was unclear,

Offered your hands when the world turned cold,

In your gaze, I found the strength to rise,

A reminder that my worth was more than gold.

Through the echoes of my struggles,

Your presence lingered, steadfast and true,

You painted my fears with colors of hope,

Transforming shadows into hues anew.

To those who cheered from the sidelines,

Who lifted my spirit with each gentle nudge,

Your loyalty carved a space in my heart,

A testament to the power of love and grudge.

You've been there since the very beginning,

A chorus of support in the symphony of my life,

With every note you played, you gave me wings,

Encouragement that cuts through the strife.

So here's my thank you, a humble tribute,

To the ones who believed when belief was thin,

Your faith stitched the fabric of my being,

And for that, I carry you within.

In the tapestry of my story, you are woven,

Threads of connection, vibrant and bright,

Thank you for seeing the artist, the man,

For being the stars in my darkest night.

ABOUT THE AUTHOR

Demii Unsylie / The Artist Leochi

Raised in Marietta, GA, by way of Louisville, KY, is a man who has lived many lives. With the soul of a modern-day ronin, he wields his pen like a katana, carving his path through life and cutting through the layers of truth and experience. His journey has been shaped by countless roads traveled, diverse experiences, and the knowledge gained from navigating the complexities of existence in America.

As a man who has weathered the storms and challenges familiar to many, Demii turns his focus to the art of storytelling. His writing sheds light on the mindset of a man facing the struggles of life, offering a raw, authentic perspective that resonates with the reality of the human condition. Now, as an author, Demii channels his experiences into words, crafting poetry and narratives that explore identity, belonging, resilience, and the beauty found in life's imperfections.

Each piece he writes is a testament to his journey—a mission to reveal his truth, not just for himself but for those who seek connection through shared experiences. Through his work, Demii invites readers to step into his world, offering them the wisdom of a man who continues to carve his way forward, one line at a time.

ACKNOWLEDGEMENT

First and foremost, I want to thank my family for their unwavering love, patience, and understanding. To my wife, your strength and support have been the foundation upon which I've built my dreams. To my daughter, your light and laughter remind me every day why it's worth chasing after what matters. You both inspire me to be the best version of myself, and without you, none of this would be possible.

To my parents, you have given me the tools to navigate this world and the courage to pursue my dreams. To my aunts, uncles, cousins, siblings, and in-laws, your support and love have been constant through every season. You have shaped me in more ways than I can express, and I am grateful for each of you. Every family gathering, every shared memory, has played a part in the person I've become. Thank you for standing by me, for seeing my potential, and for reminding me that family is more than just blood—it's the ties we choose to nurture.

To My RED CIRCLE, you know who you are. We may not share blood, but we are bound by something even stronger. In times of triumph and despair, you have been my rock, my sanctuary. We have built this circle from trust, loyalty, and resilience. Thank you for being my chosen family, for standing beside me through it all, and for giving me the strength to rise when life knocked me down. This book is as much yours as it is mine.

To my friends and colleagues, your encouragement and belief in my work have been invaluable. Thank you for every conversation, every moment of advice, and every word of kindness that helped shape this book. You've all been an integral part of this journey, and I'm forever grateful.

To the teachers, mentors, and artists who have crossed my path, thank you for sharing your wisdom and for challenging me to grow. Your influence has left an indelible mark on my life and my writing.

Lastly, to the readers—both new and those who have followed my work from the beginning—thank you for your time, your curiosity, and your openness to the stories I share. This book is for you as much as it is for me.

Thank you to everyone who has been a part of this journey. Your faith in me fuels my passion, and for that, I will always be grateful.